How to Win His Heart

An Essential Guide for Getting the Love You Want

by Anthony Corzen

Table of Contents

Introduction...1

Chapter 1: What Men Want...7

Chapter 2: Understanding Why Love Dims..............15

Chapter 3: Taking the First Step 21

Chapter 4: Adding Warmth 27

Chapter 5: Adding Heat 33

Conclusion...37

Introduction

You've given your heart to someone, and you know he's the man for you. With each look, he tugs at your emotions, and a warm gesture from him has the power to make your day. But try as you might, you feel as if you love him far more than he does you — and that's a painful position to be in.

Perhaps he's just not "there" yet, or if you're already in long-term relationship, perhaps he just doesn't love you with the same degree of passion that he once did. There may have been a time when his heartstrings were at your fingertips too, when he would smile at your mere presence. But over time, you've slowly watched that love and excitement in his eyes dim, until its embers now glow in place of a once roaring fire.

And you keep asking yourself... Have I done something wrong? Could there be someone else? Why doesn't he seem to love me anymore?

The good news is that you have the power to do something about it, and this book was written to help guide you through the steps. As long as you're willing to put in a little effort and turn a critical eye to your relationship, you can actually influence his emotions and rev up his feelings for you.

While this process may not be easy because you'll have to face some harsh realities; the solutions themselves will be quite simple to put in place. Since he's your man – the love of your life – I can guarantee you that this journey is going to be will be well worth the effort.

So, if you're ready to capture his heart and inflame his love for you like never before, becoming the sole object of his emotions and desires, then let's get started!

Chapter 1: What Men Want

By and large, it's far easier to generalize about what teenage boys want, than what men want. However, while those generalized desires may change as boys turn into men, they don't always disappear—nor do they translate into turn-offs. By this I mean, if boys like thinking of attractive and curvaceous women available at their every beck and call while fantasizing during suspiciously long showers, they will continue to feel the same way deep down, well into adulthood. And how do we know this for certain? Because, while the mental processes of an adult male are more sophisticated and nuanced than a teenager's, it's not the "mind" that is responsible for these fantasies to begin with.

Now, why are we speaking of fantasies when this book means to deal with emotions? Because therein lies your answer. Men want a fantastical life—each and every single one of them, and most of them will never admit this out loud if asked by their partners. Again, why? Because, contrary to popular belief, most men aren't jerks. They will never admit to wishing that their life had more fantasy than it currently does, because they know that this is a rather large expectation to fulfill, and may well end up upsetting their partner more than bringing any joy or positivity to their collective lives. So, they would rather lie to your face, and speak of the satisfaction of growing up into a responsible adult with commitments to fulfill. Yeah, because that sounds about as thrilling as spending your summers at Accountancy Camp. However, unless your man was raised in an extremely unstable environment and *craves* normalcy, men often want to have grander emotions in their lives—for example, they want to be regarded by their women as their heroes, in a sense. Yes, it may be silly, but that doesn't make it any less accurate.

While different men vary in their opinion on surprises, pleasant or otherwise, they like to have a sense of thrill and excitement in their lives. However, speed bumps in their love life usually start when they aren't getting those adrenaline rushes from their partners. In such cases, the *thing* which makes them feel most alive usually shifts from their partner to either work, hobbies, or other men and women as friends and/or lovers. *This* is what you've lost, and what you need to reclaim above all else.

Also, while men don't like to be thanked for actions which they took for sake of other's happiness, they don't appreciate having their contributions overlooked or written off as stuff they are meant to do. Therefore, while women who settle into the role of long-term partners often feel the need to keep correcting their men for their own good, or even dictate laws or rules in order to preserve the long-term health and well-being of their husbands or boyfriends—it's a recipe for disaster. After all, unless you're counting on Stockholm syndrome to do your job for you, one can hardly fall in love with one's jailer. Moreover, while psychiatrists gleefully rehash the old tropes that men often choose women who have some dominant qualities of their mothers—no sane, balanced man would want their mother around all the time. It would cramp their freedom and selfhood way too much.

Instead, what men worth their salt want is a partner who can make them feel special—and that's what it's really all about. However, while that may be a sentiment easily expressed in a single sentence, putting it into practice is far more complicated.

Men like partners who are kind and caring to them and the people they care about, and possibly even strangers who need a bit of kindness in their lives—but who are still self-reliant enough to handle themselves if their man isn't around. They like women who have a sense of adventure when it comes to sex, and have no trouble deferring to their man in bed. Yet again, this doesn't mean that they are in any way *less* than their man, but that they have no trouble taking control from time to time or even fighting for themselves. Sex in itself becomes an activity that should be equally sought out by both partners, rather than by one or the other most of the time. Thus, instead of a chore where both partners have to walk a thousand steps to ring a metaphorical "bell" in their partner, it becomes a regular game where playing is more fun than keeping score.

Moreover, men like women who are inquisitive and curious about the world, and are ready and willing to engage their men whenever the opportunity avails itself through stimulating conversation. However, that isn't the same thing as being a know-it-all who constantly defends his/her position against all evidence or odds. It is also not the same thing as patronizing or insulting one's partner's opinions in discussions, nor berating them with egotistical tinges of superiority.

While men do enjoy a bit of jealousy in their women, it's only to the point when it's still fun, intimate, and personal. However, the moment the jealousy turns into negativity, undue suspicion or questioning, overwhelming insecurity, or unnecessary possessiveness aimed at people around their man—this trait quickly turns into a burden.

Above all, men want women to enter and enhance their existing lives—but not overturn or substitute them. For many women, the idea that their man would continue prioritizing other matters or people in the same league as them seems insulting, since they're the partners and should receive the highest attention—but that's a baffling notion in practice. After all, while you may hold the strings to their emotions, there are others who evoke different sorts of emotions in them as well—loyalty, camaraderie, mentorship, etc.—and so are quite important within their support structure outside of you as well.

Continuing along the same line, men do understand that they may find themselves in erroneous positions from time to time. However, the way women handle those errors often determine the depth of their man's attachment to them. If women act annoyed, arrogant, or in any way to suggest superiority, the initial sheepishness from having made a mistake evaporates rather quickly (I'm not discussing infidelity or any earth-shattering errors here; more akin to picking up the wrong grocery item or forgetting something rather small), and quickly turns to bitterness and irritation over time.

In short, men want a hot, interesting, intelligent woman who doesn't mind showing the depth of her attraction to them, doesn't berate or nag, but is instead kind, caring, compassionate, and patient, loves experimenting in bed and relinquishing control without begrudging it, and gives her man ego boosts whenever needed. That's all. It's so simple. Such an easy task, right? And yes, I'm being sarcastic. However, it *is* the truth. As I said, men want fantasies. And if you wish to hold his heart forever, you'll have to work your best to provide it.

Chapter 2: Understanding Why Love Dims

Now, just as there are several limitations to generalizing what men want, there are equally as many limits on being able to ascertain the exact reasons behind the dimming of love's fire. That being said, there are a few significant ones which nonetheless plague most love lives.

The first one which is usually seen is this—ego battles. Today's world is a battle between the sexes, with the weight given to gender identities within a couple adding more load to the shoulders of an average relationship. Love has been left behind as the most important criteria for potential success in a relationship, and instead it is "respect". And the reason said word is in quotation marks is because this respect surpasses the traditional definition of the term. Having love is now less important than many an arbitrary subjective wish that are being equated with "respect", such as me wanting to be introduced to a partner's friend within the first sixty seconds— because otherwise it means my partner is either ashamed of me, doesn't respect me, or is hiding something from me."

However, the problem with this incessant demand for respect in long-term relationships often means that you're not even giving the other person a chance to respect you in their own way. If one person sets the bar for a certain quality, and doesn't discuss this interpretation of said quality with the partner, it usually ends up in more fights than seen by Attila the Hun. However, the understanding that the origin of said fights lies in the need for respect is quickly forgotten as additional ego battles ensue and build over this foundation. This is often seen in relationships where one partner or the other has gotten too comfortable, and is now starting to take the partner's presence for granted, or one of them carries insecurities from previous liaisons where respect was truly lacking. In this manner, the need to fulfill the call of one's insecurities by disallowing your loved ones to provide those sensations and qualities in their own way is a sure-shot way to throw a bucket of water on love's raging bonfire.

Another way lies in a woman's interaction with her partner's family and friends. Now, you may not always understand why other people, barring your man's family, could be considered vital to his life as well; it's because you consider yourself to be the only truly permanent part of his life. You've already assigned everyone else to the temporary pile, sometimes just because you don't personally get along particularly well with them and consider it a partner's duty to place you in your rightful position at the top of the Christmas tree and discard the rest. However, every person has multiple facets to their personality, which aren't always visible to the ones they love but may come freely in front of other social circles. This, in particular, is interpreted as insulting to women who expect their partners to share every single portion of themselves with their girlfriend/spouse. However, this may not always be a conscious thought or action on behalf of men, and may be born in response to their surroundings rather than any decision per se. Regardless, this still represents aspects of their personality that need an outlet, which may cause a sense of unfulfillment if left unchecked (Yet again, I'm not addressing infidelity as a personality aspect). Therefore, if you don't treat their friends and family as warmly as you can, you may be in for trouble at some point in the future.

The dimming of passions or their absence altogether is often a symptom of something greater and deeper which is unbalanced within the relationship. It never crops up if both partners have their guards down and can freely be vulnerable in the company of their better halves. However, if that isn't true for your partner—as in you feel like they're starting to erect walls around themselves—this may not necessarily be how they treat everyone, and may sometimes be specific to you. This situation in particular is often seen when women nag or berate their partners too much over every little matter. When partners forget that picking and choosing one's battles often yields the greatest success, every third interaction feels slightly strained and tense, as if the very air between the two of you was prepping for the next bout of unpleasantness. This may also be the case if your partner doesn't display signs of unpleasantness, yet your words and actions don't make them feel great about themselves.

And finally, the last and often the most common yet shallow cause for lost or dim passions is that you've grown far too comfortable and complacent within the relationship and let go of yourself. This isn't just a physical change, but a mental one as well in which your partner may no longer have been your biggest priority for a while—often seen in women after having children, or having recently battled through great academic or professional endeavors. Having sensed this fact, and having tried to deal with it for a while—your partner may have simply let himself grow slightly indifferent to matters too, as a coping mechanism. But once your partner no longer cares enough about whether you place him as your highest priority, the ever-present love is sure to dim. Now, this trait isn't limited to women, and is seen just as frequently in men. However, given that this book is aimed towards getting one's *man* to love you more, the topic shall be dealt with by keeping that perspective in mind.

Chapter 3: Taking the First Step

The very first step which needs to be taken is to get yourself back in order. Whether you've let yourself go physically, or no longer spend as much time trying to beautify yourself for your partner, or even if you still do but haven't seen as strong a response from him as in the past—it's time to buck up and take it to the next level. However, do so in a manner which doesn't draw his attention. The impression which you want him to have isn't that you're working to get his attention back, but of you getting more beautiful and attractive each day in front of his eyes—making him question how stupid he may be to have taken someone as gorgeous as you for granted. This would be far more effective than if he figured you were to try to re-ignite something stronger in him, since that would just lead him to question whether he truly feels enough for you anymore—and that's a question you *really* don't want to bring up in his mind. However, if you'd heard him complain about you not being attracted to him anymore or at least acting like it in the past, or not caring enough about his attraction towards you, or that *you* were the one losing interest in your collective sex life because you had other priorities, giving him clues that you're doing this for him would get you better results.

Anyway, if you feel less physically fit than before, or still feel as if you can do more before reaching your optimal figure, join a gym or include fitness routines within your schedule while at home. This prospect isn't all that hard to undertake nowadays with YouTube, and you can easily find exercise regimes which fit your schedules and the space you live in. However, before doing so, I must also emphasize that this isn't an excuse to let out your insecurities and question whether you're beautiful enough for him. Remember this—if he wasn't physically attracted to you, he wouldn't have been with you in the first place. Therefore, every suggestion and course of improvement here isn't a critique on your beauty or your behavior in a relationship—these are simply ways for you to *improve* your game, and enhance your chances of firmly capturing his heart.

The next step that needs to be taken is to change the way you look right now. Think back to the last time your man was truly passionate about you. At that time, did you have a particular hairstyle which he loved, or even a style of make-up? Or did he appreciate whenever you changed up your look—possibly even changing entire hairdos every once in a while? If he had a favorite hairstyle, is that still the case, or has he moved on and given you that same look of passion for another style?

By asking yourself such questions, you can ascertain whether he loved a particular look on you which he hasn't seen in a while, or even if he loved it whenever you changed your looks drastically but hadn't done so for a while. By answering these queries, you can determine whether it would be best for you to try a new look altogether, or to return to an old favorite. However, since he no longer responds to the same things that he once did, my advice would be to try and experiment with a new look altogether—one rather different from anything you've tried before. This would allow your man to see you in an entirely new light, and to appreciate everything your looks and beauty have to offer through a fresh perspective.

After working on your looks, the next step would be fixing your wardrobe. Again, this isn't an opportunity to get out and purchase different variations of the same kinds of clothes you've always bought. Instead, the idea here is to go out and experiment with entirely new dressing styles. By exploring new options for yourself, not only are you presenting an entirely new version of you, you are also hinting at your newly-revived (or simply new) experimental nature. This in particular would be useful in igniting your man's passions because it would firstly allow him to look at you in a completely different way, and remind himself of the reason which led to him fall for you from the very beginning. Secondly, this would hint at times of change, which would be a break from routine, and would pose as a sign of better things to come.

If you haven't recently done so, try searching for a new scent for yourself as well. Most women love staying true to a certain type of scent which they like for rather long periods of time, even if the brands of said scents become more and more expensive. However, as you mature and grow, there may be other scents which may complement you better than your original one. And there's no real way for to find out unless you go out and look for it.

The last thing that you need to take care of is the sense of touch which you impart. While your fitness regime would change the way you feel in his arms, you should also work on the way your skin feels when he runs his fingers along it. As we get lost in our personal and professional lives, taking care of our skin, hygiene, and grooming sometimes gets increasingly difficult. Precious self-grooming routines and schedules get lost by the wayside as real-life responsibilities shriek for priority. At the very least, if you can't afford changing your lotion to more expensive ones or taking longer personal "spa" times, start taking milk baths by mixing in six parts of water for every one part of milk. This will give your skin a much smoother texture while moisturizing it.

Through these changes, you can enhance the sense of smell, touch, and sight, which you impart to your partner. Even though you may have been beautiful before, these changes will not only take your beauty to the next level and turn your partner's head again; the experimentation will not only rejuvenate you, but will also give you a renewed sense of who you are as a person today.

Chapter 4: Adding Warmth

After changing the way your physical attributes seduce your partner's senses, it's time to work on how you make him *feel*. While many men may have difficulties expressing softer emotions or talking about how they feel—it's still erroneous to assume that they don't understand their own emotions. Mostly because such an understanding of men's emotions rose from men not wanting to talk about their feelings, they found that feigning ignorance would be far easier to get people off their back than trying to explain *why* talking about feelings was a pain.

Before we start, let's make one thing clear—your devotion to your partner isn't under debate here. If you did not care about your partner, you wouldn't be here trying to find better ways to fight for his love. However, even when people are perfectly justified in their sense of concern for others, and have the perfect message that would help others in their endeavors, worries, or problems—the *tone* of the message is extremely, and often just as important as its content. Therefore, this section will deal with improving the way you interact with your partner.

As I mentioned before, one reason why the love may have dimmed is that many women interact in ways which make their partners feel bad about themselves and who they are as people, and the kinds of choices they make (again, not discussing infidelity or other such issues), rather than simply solving the problem or error which may have risen. Therefore, if you wish to ask your partner for help, wish to offer advice, or interact with him in any way, make sure that your tone first conveys warmth and understanding before all else. Don't let him forget that the person who's speaking to him loves him intensely. If you think that would weaken your message, you're sorely mistaken. Instead, he would be far more likely to listen to you without prejudice, conflict, or ego issues *because* you decided to forego them and take a warmer tone instead.

Even if you wish to advise him on something which you believe may be of value, don't do so in a manner which would make him feel foolish—but rather make him feel strengthened by your support towards him. Think of a general being advised by his/her staff, and that's the scenario which you need to recreate. If you help him while still letting him feel in charge of a situation, you'll have his ear and his respect till the end of time. Instead, most women try to turn everything into teaching moments where driving the point home till it's acknowledged becomes the priority—but that just leaves most men wondering if they're truly supported or simply have someone barking orders at them from behind. Don't nag or criticize—instead, your priority should be to inform, rather than bask in the glory of your own intellect. If you change your tone, even if you barely change the message, you'll automatically see an improvement in your interaction. Support, and don't be in a rush to contradict. If your man decides on something which you know to be entirely or partially wrong from your perspective, take a few minutes to understand their reasoning first. If you still find the decision to be faulty, inform them of it without seeming like you don't trust their judgment.

One easy way I've found for partners to deal with such situations is to say one positive thing first, followed by the criticism or question—and this method has been extremely successful between couples I've helped in the past. By first trying to find one good thing to say about his input/decision/opinion, you force yourself to step into his shoes, rather than simply hearing his reasoning behind the step. Not only does it give me better insight into his alternative point of view, but it also allows him to feel as if your minds are in sync on the subject—that you have his back, and *do* understand what he wishes to achieve with this step.

By addressing the criticism only after responding positively, you allow the creation of a safe space within which the conversation can expand, without your partner feeling as if you don't value his opinions. Once this bond of trust is strengthened, he would be more likely to respond to criticism objectively, rather than take it personally as a shot at his ego or intellect. It also allows him to look past the good points of said opinion or decision from his own perspective, and explore the next steps of figuring out the downsides of it without feeling like a chump.

Also, if and when your partner wants to take a step or make a choice of which you don't approve, don't sulk, pout, or get emotional. Instead, try and gauge the damage going along with said decision would cause you, and then make your decision regarding it. There may be times when your partner wishes for something, even as small as a trip with his friends, which may not hamper you per se but may be inconvenient for you nonetheless. In such a case, being warm and supportive means not letting plain inconvenience dictate your behavior towards your partner, and instead deciding upon the best path to take in a mature fashion.

Lastly, regardless of whether you get along, treat the people around him with as much warmth and importance as your partner attaches to them. If they dislike you, and this is the reason for you being unable to get along, do speak with your partner and try to find the best possible way through. However, if you carry the displeasure, and simply can't be bothered with the people around him because they don't mean as much to you—you're always going to find yourself with relationship problems where your partner doesn't love you as much as you do.

Chapter 5: Adding Heat

By this point, we've worked out ways to improve your physical appearance, the way your partner perceives you as a person, and the way in which you handle your partner's selfhood and the life around him. For the final step, we'll get to work on reigniting or enhancing your intimate life. Now, without being abusive, you need to understand that every man wants someone *lustful*.

However, they don't want someone lustful in general, but one who reserves lust solely for her man's pleasure. They want someone who gives far more than what she asks for herself—because at the root of it all, every man likes being *serviced* for pleasure. An ideal woman as a long-term partner would be one whose innermost depths of sexual deviation, excitement, and interests opened up solely with and for her one true man. Again, this doesn't mean that your pleasure and satisfaction don't carry equal weight—just that, giving pleasure without asking for it in return receives far more reciprocation than constantly asking, "What about me?" The better lovers among men, as well as the men worth being with in the first place, simply respond to this one-sided pleasure-giving by upping their game as well in order to pleasure you even more without you asking for it. When the statements change from "What about me?" to "Let me take care of you," the game of sex changes from a self-centered pursuit of pleasure to an interminable cycle of reciprocation. In such a setting, the *taking* of pleasure becomes far less important than being good at *giving* it.

And pleasure is the key to everything. Yet, don't confuse pleasure with orgasms. Those are simply the end-result of pleasurable intimacy, rather than the objective. It's the entire "the journey is more important than the destination" adage all over again. Yet, it carries immense weight in this scenario. And this starts way before the actual sex even gets underway.

Therefore, the first thing that you need to do is to start sexting with your man. Yes, you heard me right. Nothing perks up a man more than receiving a picture of his partner posing provocatively for his viewing pleasures in the middle of a dreary and boring work day. Send one more towards the end when he's just leaving to get back home, and you'll find him returning quite *enthusiastically,* if you catch my drift. If you're at work at the same time, and you send him these pictures from your office (from a restroom or whatever else), that would just be an icing on the cake. The unspoken message he would get along with the picture would be "I can't wait for you to get back home to show you how badly I need you *right now.*"

And nothing else would get his motor running quite the same way as that bold-faced display of lust.

The second thing which you need to do is to ask him about his fantasies. Now, most long-term relationships do pass a point early on when partners ask about each other's present fantasies. But that's not your objective. You need to inquire about his fantasies when he was a young, horny teenager. These would be rather more detailed and fantastical, born out of raging hormones and periods of sought-out isolation in a simpler time when life wasn't regarded as cynically. If you manage to satisfy the teenager inside him, you'll have successfully distinguished yourself as the best lover imaginable. Not just that, you'll also incentivize him to start thinking along such lines again—and you would literally be the only thing, person, or allowance of circumstance which would have given him permission to do so in his growing responsibility-filled adulthood. Furthermore, this time his fantasies would be squarely rooted with *you* at the center. Not only would you thus be playing for his heart, but you would be gaining control of that hormone-addled teenager inside as well which every man buries deep under the rockslide of adult reality, out of sight but never forgotten.

Conclusion

As you must have discovered for yourself, *getting* the perfect partner is actually much easier than keeping him happy and in love with you over long periods. But this is where a strong relationship distinguishes itself from weaker ones. Again, to clarify, there exists no strong relationship today which had smooth sailing from start to end. Smooth sailing simply means that the mother of all storms has yet to hit. Instead, every strong relationship has been built on the foundations of *several* great storms faced together. As long as the embers of feelings survive, they can be fanned into a great roaring fire yet again.

However, understand this well—these steps will require you to push aside all of your personal misgivings, sense of morality, instinctive decisions, etc. You will need to push aside your natural reactions, and pursue only those actions which would bring him back to you—come what may, and at any price. But don't take yourself past a point of no return. I've known men *and* women exploit partners in such situations to enter sexual forays *outside* their bond together, with partners going along simply to please them. If you think that anything *outside* the two of you would change the way you think about yourself forever, draw a sharp line there. However, as long as the action or direction only involves the two of you, throw out your self-inscribed boundaries. You will need to pledge everything to make this happen in a permanent way, which will avoid such a situation from *ever* coming up again. Otherwise, going through these efforts would be pointless if you had to redo them once every few years.

Therefore, proceed on this path only if you believe that you can push aside your own needs and wishes for the time being. The up side is that you can always build your wishes, dreams, aspirations, and desires back into the foundation of your rejuvenated relationship once your man is wholly yours. However, if even that temporary sacrifice seems too big of a step, you may want to rethink whether or not *you* are ready to take these steps for him, and whether you still feel as strongly for him.

Lastly, the instructions in this book are meant to change your behavior to bring you closer to a middle path in order to shock your man back into recognizing the various gifts which you bring into the relationship. However, if you've always been docile or servile, it's time to take charge of your life. In such a case, changing your physical appearance and look should be a great start at making your own mark. Sexting as well, initiated by you, as well as the desire to enact his fantasies without prompting would be choices that you make on your own. But, beyond that, you need to start voicing your opinions and speaking up when you have something to contribute. Moreover, initiate important discussions on your own, instead of waiting for him to do so. Assert a confident outlook, and take some time off to spend with your friends if you didn't do so before. While a docile personality may have suited your previous shyness, and there may be a part of your man which respects the quiet strength of a quiet and soft-spoken personality, such mild-mannered attributes often become *bland* quite fast as well. Especially since it means that you would often overturn your own choices and preferences in favor of his own, leaving you rather tasteless as a personality on the outside. So, let your inner being come out, and watch his surprise grow into admiration and affection as he gets to know the inner you—a side he has never seen before.

Most of all, if you perform these steps as if they were duties or chores you're *supposed* to perform, you *will* fall flat on your face. Open up your heart and body to your man, take a leap of faith, and have *fun* on this explorative journey. You'll come out on the other end far stronger as an individual than before. I guarantee it!

Finally, I'd like to thank you for purchasing this book! If you found it helpful, I'd greatly appreciate it if you'd take a moment to leave a review on Amazon. Thank you!

Printed in Great Britain
by Amazon